Church Folks
The Real Deal

Church Folks
The Real Deal

Mama P.

The Regency
Publishers

Copyright © 2022 by Mama P.

All rights reserved. No part of this book may be reproduced in any form or by any electronic or mechanical means, including information storage and retrieval systems, without permission in writing from the author and publisher, except by reviewers, who may quote brief passages in a review.

ISBN: 978-1-957724-25-6 (Paperback Edition)
ISBN: 978-1-957724-24-9 (Hardcover Edition)
ISBN: 978-1-957724-26-3 (E-book Edition)

Book Ordering Information

Phone Number: 315-537-3088 ext 1007
Email: info@theregencypublishers.com
The Regency Publishers, US
www.theregencypublishers.us

Printed in the United States of America

Church Folks Christians
Which One Are You or Both?

GOD is a spirit of Peace, Joy, Love and Happiness.....not a spirit of confusion.

People will show you what they want you to see.

It is so time consuming living a fake life trying to impress people. Be real in whatever you do especially in praising the lord. God made us, this double life your living is all your doing.

One day we were at the church working and a middle-age man came by depressed and in tears. He said "please I need someone to pray for me", a member told the young man, you have to come back later when the Pastor come in. I said, really we can pray for him ourselves. The same God that hears the Pastor can also hear us. After praying for him his spirit was lifted and he couldn't stop thanking us. He gave a thank you so much and he left and was on his way.

One by one we are falling along the wayside, minding everyone's business except our own.

Some people are so good in quoting scripture by scripture. They talk so fast and bring out words so quick until they forgot to listen to what the words are saying.

If you are treating someone bad, remember that you will someday reap what you sow.

There are people that believe that they're perfect. These persons are living in denial. No one is perfect.

Those who sit in the pulpit is not free from sin and probably sin more than the ones in the pews.

While in church one should dress accordingly not to bring attention to themselves or others alike.

Church Folks Christians
Which One Are You or Both?

You said the LORD called Jane but, how do you know, what are the qualifications for this position?

You said that the LORD called you to preach, did he say to you that you were call to preach, how you don't know he didn't call you to minister to the people of the streets. Everything is not handed to you on a silver platter. The LORD does not tell you to stay within a building you must go out among those that are lost.

Were you not lost before you were found? Pray before you step out into this world, everything is different. There is no day or night that is the same.

Everyone has to remember that all of us have obstacles to cross. We will go through trials and tribulations in our lifetime. There will be good times as well as bad. Through it all, will come victory. You have to remember where you came from in order to know where you are going. No beginning, no ending, think about it. This is life and we must go through, to get to the breakthrough.

If you don't want anything in life then you won't get anything in life. Before you go casting stone against someone as a Church Folk/Christian, clean around your own front door.

Getting our life right with GOD is a must. Everything that is going on around the world is not of GOD. The enemy has a GOD also and he sends havoc all around. The killing, robbing and committing suicide is of the enemy.

Men going out there attacking young ladies and men. The work of the enemy, this person needs help. These young ladies seeking older men affection mostly for money but still selling their bodies for money. These ladies have low self-esteem and of course, they need love, they need help. ChurchFolks/Christians we need to help with the young ladies and young men. We need to set an example for them to follow.

Church Folks Christians
Which One Are You or Both?

Some Church Folks – Christians preach a good sermon but where are they, when you really truly need them? Church Folks – Christians are needed to visit the sick and shut-in, visit the prisons. Yes, I write Church Folks-Christians because some of them are just that. I did not say GOD did not call them but, they get weak also. They are not to be put on highpedestals. They also fall short of the glory of the LORD. They sit and talk about people even though their life is not clean. Some Church Folks/Christians rule and disrespect their significant other, not of GOD. Some Christians/Church Folks are very controlling. We need to continue praying for one another sincerely. I don't care how much we dress-up for church in our new attire you are still not an angel no matter what. Get right with GOD and do it now. You can stand before a church congregation on a Sunday and on Monday you are meeting someone at a hotel that belongs to someone else…you have just committed adul- tery among other things. Please don't think no one saw you, no matter what, GOD is always watching. Never give into your sins, your sins will guarantee you a seat in Hell. You got to care.

Some people would rather you turn a truth into a lie to make you feel better but all you would be doing is living a lie. If you were perfect you would not be here on earth. The LORD can't use perfection you must have a spot or wrinkle. You must be able to go through in order for him to bless you. All of us have anger problems but, we must get through them.

If anything you are nothing but a fake, lying deceitful Church Folk-Christian. They say the truth will set you free. You must acknowledge your shortcomings,

- You must know what you lack in your life not the material things either…

- You must know that the married man or woman you are sleeping with is married

Church Folks Christians
Which One Are You or Both?

This is what I'm hearing in both instances so what all of us is married okay!! So you'll don't care then one day you will have to give an account. If all you have is your body to sell for money then, I'm sorry. Your name will go on the sick list because you need help. How do you sleep at night? No conscience. How do you expect your children to respect you if you don't respect yourself?

Church Folks, real Christians please we need to pray for the broken hearted. We sit and judge but we really don't know the beginning. What is your beginning? Sweep around your front, back and side door.

Church Folks/Christians, you said the man loves you but you and him make love in the car. Baby, he doesn't love nor respect you. You are only his side chick. Cut him off, you are more important than that. Young ladies and young men, stop selling yourself cheap, you are not for sale.

Church Folks/Christians some of you would probably never help someone that is homeless because of his or her demeanor or maybe because you think that he or she is beneath you. Remember that one day this could be you. It is always nice and a privilege to help someone when you can. Don't be selfish for one day you may need someone to help you.

Church Folks/Christians finds it a joy locking the ministers out the church just know that sooner or later you won't think it's something to laugh about when it hits home. Be very careful what you do.

If you can't think for yourself, you better ask the Almighty for guidance. If you want to be respected then you give it. Don't ever disrespect the Pastor or any adult older than yourself. You will have to give account sooner than you think. This is not something to laugh or joke about. Mom or Dad can't get you in Heaven.

Church Folks Christians
Which One Are You or Both?

Some Church Folks or Christians together would rather drink and party themselves crazy. There is more to life than drinking alcohol and I don't mean rubbing alcohol either. There is a reason that you are drinking and whatever pain you are in will not go away. After the alcohol has worn off the pain will still exist. You got to find the LORD and seek him for yourself. No he is not lost but you are. Some people have self-esteem issues be- cause they don't love themselves. When you find yourself and love yourself you will find the person that is worthy of you, the LORD will place you together.

Church Folks/Christians someone in Church just asked you to stand with her in Prayer by marching in the church seven (7) times and some of you don't even move after an awesome sermon. GOD is not pleased with a lot of you. You don't ever know when you are going to need someone; you better mind how you treat people.

Church Folks Christians
Which One Are You or Both?

GOD wants to be served wholeheartedly

Everyone should get their own personal house in order in this instance your heart...

God walked right for us. GOD stood for the right things.

Call GOD's promise back to him when you have your conversation with him. Continue crying out to the LORD in spite of what looks like. GOD has seen your tears. You ought to be careful with your words because it has power. This world today is going crazy. When you think you know more than GOD, I advise you to go in your secret closet and pray. You haven't started praising GOD until someone gets on your nerve. Can I trust you when I'm catching HELL? LORD when you start passing out Blessings please, please don't forget about me.

I love being by myself. I will not beg someone to be my friend. I will not buy someone to be my friend. I love the LORD and he knows my heart. He knows all about me. I don't have to be phony or fake. If I can help someone in any way I will. You cannot make me do what you want me to do. I have a mind of my own.

We have a member that has been missing from our church almost two (2) years no one seem to know what happened to him. As many churches that we have in the community we couldn't raise enough money to help him or to find out what happened to him. Where is the love? Where is the love? Why do we have all of these churches in the community? Some of these church doors need to be closed. People need to really come together and have church.

The Pastors at some of these churches, the members dislike them. They just put up with them. LORD, please step in and do a turn over like only you can. LORD, please send down one of those old time religion ceremony. You choose the speaker.

Church Folks Christians
Which One Are You or Both?

It is wrong for people to know that things are wrong and they band together knowing it was wrong. Depending on who's doing the wrong they go along with it. They will have to pay for it later in life.

Church Folks/ Christians do they really love themselves, they have troubles and testimonies like everyone else. They show some kind of love for the children in the schools. Where is the love for the elderly? In some point of our life we are really confuse.

Church is not a showplace to see who can preach, pray, shout or sing better than the other. Church should be about love. I ask again, where is the love?

Church Folks/Christians makes promises they don't keep. LORD please break all these chains and generational curses.

Jesus is real to me. Oh yeah, yes He gave us the victory! So many people doubt it. I can't live without him. That is why I love him so...he is so real to me. This is no time for playing church but it is time for praying. You can go to church seven (7) days a week it still won't grant you a seat in the Kingdom. You were given a gift okay use it wisely. You go to see the sick or not this is not of GOD. You go to some and not others this is not of GOD.

You can go to church on Sunday and soon as church is over, you are out the door. GOD is not pleased with this action.

You go home after church pop a lid off a can or open a bottle of wine, Christians and church folks do this. Just know you are not fooling anyone but yourself because GOD sees and knows it all. The Lord is my light and my Salvation whom shall I fear except the enemies who calls themselves your friend.

Church Folks Christians
Which One Are You or Both?

The Fruit of the Spirit – when the spirit of GOD is within someone it is a light that cannot be hidden.

Jesus didn't die so that we would come to church. Jesus died so that we would become the church.

Everyone is worried about everyone's soul but is your soul anchored in the Lord?

They're some people in church that they know everything even more than GOD himself. GOD doesn't need anyone to imitate him.

There's a lot of wolves out there in sheep's clothing. Some of us need to walk around with a mirror in our purse or briefcase.

Because you have a beautiful voice and can sing doesn't mean you will make it into the kingdom...search your heart.

Because you can pray doesn't mean you will be given the key to the kingdom...search your heart.

Church folks are always giving each other compliments and half of the time they're lying, sugar coating instead of telling the truth. A lie, denial or fabricating won't get you in the kingdom. We need to be honest with one another.

Sure you can sing but singing won't get you in. Praying, you did a great job but while you were praying, were you listening, really listening?

You can stand in the pulpit and preach the word. As you were preaching did you place yourself in these situations? Please Lord, show us the right way. Church Folks, the Lord has bless you, who have you blessed today? Have you given someone a hug today? Church folks, some of you are mean, selfish living a lie in the church and out. The Lord has given all of us a gift and we need to use it wisely.

Church Folks Christians
Which One Are You or Both?

Everyone that cries out to the Lord won't make it into heaven! The Heavenly Gates. Some church folks I must say you can never tell me right from wrong because of your reactions. How, I saw you being disrespectful to your Superior. You must know that before some of you leave here you must give account for your actions. Yes, God is good all the time.

Church folks/Christians they're not hard to figure out at all. They're so transparent. You can't go to them for anything especially a listening ear and show love. They have certain people that they do for and some that they ignore.

GOD is love. Church folks/Christians are not now if you read this and get highly upset is because the words touched a nerve. Instead of getting upset or angry just move on and straighten yourself out.

There is no one on earth that is perfect. If you want to say that you are let me tell you right up front that you are in denial and you just told the biggest lie.

I had qualms about this book but this is something I asked my heavenly father about and He is helping me along the way.

As an usher you come in contact with all types of spirits. We must be very careful. At funerals some ushers are so mean and yet, they're the same one that asks the LORD for guidance well, the enemy has his lord also. I rebuke all this meanness and anger bitterness out of GOD's domain (house). You want to get paid for preaching the word please show me in the Bible where the Lord preached for money...Lord, there is so much going on in our Father's house. The LORD sent a Pastor to be the head of the church. Please take note that the Head of the Church but the people still have a voice. Just remember that GOD is the main factor.

Church Folks Christians
Which One Are You or Both?

Some preachers will tell other preachers that they're not allowed in their church please leave or leave! They will also say that you are not allowed in my church to preach. These preachers come in and try to break the church.Do you really think this is true? Where did you get this theory from? Will there ever be a preacher that you are happy with or will you ever be happy? Remember to do things that line up with GOD - GOD isn't connected with this foolishness.

Where is your perfection degree?

Where is your intelligence as far as dealing with the church finances? You can't run the church like how you run your finances.

Church folks are so petty now run and tell that. Always trying to cause confusion within the church house. Peace be still.

I don't know how some people sleep at night with all this wickedness, within their heart. You wonder why, you were always feeling good and all of a sudden you start going downhill.Search your heart, search yourself.

You have some people in church that wants to always be the center of attention. It is not working. You need to let the LORD use you and you get in where you fit in. Let someone else have a chance.

No church, no denomination is better than the other. There is no competition between none. Your Pastor cannot run your life, can't control you. Your Pastor can't send you to heaven or hell but we can. Read your Bible for yourself. We are not perfect if we were we would not be living here on earth. You would have gone on to be with the Lord. If you have done wrong to someone please go and apologize. In church if someone doesn't like you, you can kiss their butt all you want, it won't change anything.

Church Folks Christians
Which One Are You or Both?

There should be love shown at all times. If I know someone don't care for me I separate myself. You meet them and in a second they change. Nothing for the better, either the majority of them is fake, fake, fake...Don't ever do things to please man. Turn to the LORD because he won't ever let you down. You don't need a platform to be heard. You can tell a person this or that unless you have tried on the same shoes and it fit leave it alone. You have so many judgements and advice and don't really know a thing at all.

You should love your neighbors as you love yourself. Some of us have so much and we just refuse to help someone in need. This is called a selfish kind of love. As the Lord bless us we are supposed to help others.

Church folks/Christians how dare you put someone out of your church because of the way he chose to go in life. We need to pray for one another instead of judging them. Who gives us this right, surely not our Heavenly Father.

In life we need to take one step at a time two steps will make us fall. Always show love wherever we go. If you can give with love in mind. When GOD gave up his only son, he was not thinking about himself he was showing love and putting all of us first.

I have visited churches in the past and all of them are run differently, some of them are confusing the Almighty big time. Not one person runs the church except the almighty. In churches we have different personalities. Different ways of thinking, and different ways of showing love. Some are even confused about right and wrong. The definitions never changes.

God's love is never-ending. He rocks us to sleep every night and sing lullabies to get us started each day.

Church Folks Christians
Which One Are You or Both?

God doesn't do groups or clicks. God doesn't have favorites. Every Christian/ Church folks has to stand before a JUST GOD for themselves as yourself, so you better mind. Who are we to chastise? I'm pretty sure that none of us are living a sin-free life. Be careful of casting the first stone because it can come back to haunt you one day. Listen to that song "Sinner-Man" it is speaking to both genders. I don't care if you preach from the pulpit, something she will whisper in your ear, are you listening to what you are saying?

Church folks/Christians just because you know how to handle church programs doesn't mean that you will have the first seat at Heaven's Gate. Whatever title you are holding at the church, you are still supposed to always respect the members and guests.

People of the cloth, if a member doesn't do as you ask rather good or bad, please don't get angry with them they have their own opinions. You have no right in putting no one of the Lord's pulpit if you angry about something. Before you act, pray about it.

Church Folks Christians
Which One Are You or Both?

GOD gets all the Glory! The truth better be in you.

    A Church folk is someone who just goes to church just to be going. Does this ring a bell within you?

A church folk go to church to be a model with the MAC make- up, the Maybelline to the mascara. Do you know him for the pardon of your sin? Do you love the LORD from your heart? Do you love your fellowman/woman? Most of all, do you love yourself? Do you love your neighbor as yourself?

The LORD loves all of us; do you believe that he is well- pleased with the life that you are living? Are you please with yourself?

We don't go to church to model our attire but to worship the Almighty. We sit in judgement of other people but we really need to do an inventory of ourselves. We don't need to compete for GOD's love because he loves us all equally. There is no comparison. The LORD loves wholeheartedly. He wants us to love another.

I want you to go out and purchase a small mirror and keep it in your purse and every time you gossip or talk about someone, take your mirror out and look into it not to ask for a wish but to check yourself out. Are you without sin? Are you perfect? No I answered this because, no one is. Are you even cute? Don't be casting any stones.

    In growing up practically every little child in the community grew up in church. My daddy always had a club and he was the owner but my mom and I were the ones in the club. Daddy was in the house in his bed.

    Growing up there was always a lot of churches in the community like, Charity A.M.E; Stewart Chapel UMC; Zion UMC; New Hope UMC; St. Phillip; Miracle Revival;Rev.

Church Folks Christians
Which One Are You or Both?

Coaxum Church and Rev. Bennett Church. We were never short of Churches. Everyone who attends Church is not where they need to be. That is why they're called Church Folks. A lot of Church Folks get angry when you talk about the Church Folks, why are you getting so angry? Are you a Church Folk or a Christian?

There is no one that goes to church part-time or full- time can get you into the kingdom. Do not put man before the Almighty. Man will let you down everytime. The Lord, he never will.

Fulltime Church Folks attends 4-5 Sundays a month, everyday some 24 hours and part-time Church Folks attends every now and then and still don't have true religion. When you do go to church, the Church folks are so funny acting, selfish and rude including some in the pulpit that needs to step-down – you hypocrite.

I call them as I see them. So, I think some even have Alzheimer's. Lord, please let your presence be known. We need an old-time revival where we go to the altar and call on the name of Jesus. I attended a church service at one time where the Preacher said that some of us have been called to preach and some again have been called to pick peach. Well someone needs to let the peach pickers know that until you go and pick your peach and get it right, you need to fall on your knees and call on the name of the LORD.

We are living in an era now where you have another job in the church and you think that you are the preacher and know everything. Please let whoever the LORD sends do their job. We need to remember to let the LORD have his way that way is definitely not your way. The church is not Burger King where you go and you have it your way. It is God's way. The Church is not Church's Fried Chicken where everything isfast. You seek Jesus until you find the LORD.

Church Folks Christians
Which One Are You or Both?

The recipe for Deliverance starts by you asking the Lord to deliver you from all sin and evil. Where you ask for your sins to be forgiven the seen and unseen, the known and unknown. Sometimes, when we are alone we can just sit and talk to the Lord, one on one. You can do this when you are young and also when you are restless. The Days of Our Lives we need to cherish, while we search for tomorrow because sometimes tomorrow never comes. As we sit on the edge of the night we slumber into deep, despair wondering where we go from here. We always try to take things into our hands but we need to lean on God's understanding not our own. The Lord closes our eyes at different times so he opens and some he lets stay close because it is time to move on. We really need to get it together. You are not better than me and I am not better than you.

Everything that we have belongs to the Lord. We belong to the Lord. Get your stubborn behind right and do it now. Church folks get you together. Ask yourself this question, are you doing all that you can do to help another or are you just that selfish and stingy.

Please remember who gave you everything that you have. If you come across someone going through hard times don't try to be a psychiatrist and figure what the person prob- lems is just help him or her out if you can. Our Almighty will do the rest. If you did someone wrong the phrase is "I am sorry" don't you feel better. Church folks stop looking down on people unless you are helping them up. I just said hello to you and you switch your little narrow behind off, moving right along. All the Bible Studies, all the Church Services will go down in vain if you are not applying yourself properly. You standing at the door as an usher, you standing or sitting in the pulpit, you singing or standing on the choir won't get you there but Love will. You must learn to forgive yourself.

Church Folks Christians
Which One Are You or Both?

You as a church folk meeting someone's husband or wife at some hotel to have sex and bragging about it. You are a cold blooded human being, asks the Lord to forgive you. Ask the Lord to forgive you for going through your nasty ventures. Your mother is on the Steward Board and she finds out what you are doing to make money and she is ashamed and puts you out of the house. She stops going to church because she feels ashamed. Mother dear, we know you didn't raise your child to be this way. You have nothing to be ashamed of. Let the Lord fight your battles for it is not yours but the Lords.

Some of us Church Folks forget why we walk through the church doors. It is not walking down the runway model- ing our clothes and hats. We come to church to enjoy Jesus. Before we even start church we should go to the Altar and pray. We can even stay at our seats and pray. We still need to come together as one. The church is not a place to come and play church. Everyone has a gift, we need to use it, and it's not always in the pulpit. Get yourself together Church folks. Don't be jumping from church to church thinking that it will get better, the church doesn't move. Sometimes the enemygoes right along with you. The problem is you. Someone should've told you that. The church is a just a building. Sometimes we have to reach way down.

Christians feel your pain when you are going through. Church folks could care less. Church folks hear about you losing a love one, they don't care. Christians will come by to lend a helping hand. They would stand by you through it all. They would call to check on you before and after. Church folks are too busy trying to get popularity. Church folks will walk over by you and keep going; sure some Christians will do this also.

Church Folks and some Christians are alike in some cases and to be honest it's true. If so and so is preaching I don't want to go to

Church Folks Christians
Which One Are You or Both?

our church today. I will go and visit another church. Some of us are going to go to hell because of not what another person does but it's because of what you do that will keep us from getting into the kingdom.

Church Folks Christians
Which One Are You or Both?

Some Bishops, Prophets, Elders, Evangelists, Preachers and Ministers are just in the pulpit to receive money for their services. Some of you'll are not going to make it in because of that. Stop putting a price on what you say the Lord has called you to do. Some of you who preach can still work on some- one's job, do you remember how to complete job applications, if you need help, please ask. No one can stop you from making it into the kingdom but you. Stop blaming people for your short comings. Stop blaming people from seeing right through your lies and wickedness. This also a gift.

Stop judging, you didn't come into the world perfect so please don't even think that. We sin everyday rather we know it or not. In life we are going to go through things, this is how we go to the Lord for him to guide us through. Remember how Cain and Able were brothers and one was jealous of the other this is how we are today. We don't need to be but, we are.

You see how Eve's head was hard for listening to man instead of God. This is exactly how we are today. You may look down on me all you want, I will be the person that will rise again and pick you up along the way. I go to a cookout and a Church folk and Christian see me dancing, it's okay while you are talking. I am enjoying myself not only that, the Lord see everything that I'm doing and I'm not hurting anyone at all. All I can say is that you better enjoy yourself because you don't know when we will be called on home.

Church Folks and Christians leave those people spouses alone. Ask the Lord to bless you with a spouse but be very specific in your asking.

Church folks/Christians we must get it together. If you know someone needs help with paying a bill help them or move out of the way for someone else to help them. Church folks, Christians

Church Folks Christians
Which One Are You or Both?

did you ever preach and the member of the church gave you a Love Offering and you gave it back to the church? Church folks, Christians did you ever receive a Love offering and after you receive it and you looked at it later and was angry about it, because you didn't feel it was right?

Church Folks Christians
Which One Are You or Both?

Church Folks/ Christians what are you preaching for, to gain souls or to get paid. You ought to fall on your knees and ask the Lord to please forgive you of your sins. You knew exactly what you were doing and what you are in need of. Prayer changes everything including your mindset. The Lord didn't bring you this far to leave you. He'll never leave you but you will leave him. Get it together Church folks and Christians. Normally when you leave here you will be the one that sends yourself to Heaven or Hell not man. You have to decide if you want to serve man or the Lord. The decision is truly up to you.

You have to go the Lord and sing it's me, it's me, it's me Oh Lord standing in the need of prayer. Tell the Lord what you want. He's a deliverer he can deliver you from sin, surrender all to the Lord.

A lot of Church Folks/Christians want to attack the Pastors of the Church. I am pretty sure you have a lot of family matters that needs attending to leave the pastors alone. Some Church Folks and Christians can be a sheep (a little lamb) in wolves clothing ready to attack at any moment. You being, the Pastor how can you tell the congregation how to live when you sleeping with the Deacon or the Deacon's wife? How dare you?

Someone said to me that you are going to have people angry with you. I asked the Lord to direct me in my writing and if it offends someone or steps on their toes just say ouch! Be sure you apply the corrections to yourself and get it right. Enough of playing Church and all of the sugar coating and speak the truth. If you are in the pulpit and you know your soul isn't right with the Lord, step down. Do not wait for someone to tell you to step down. We are not in this world to make man happy but to get it right with GOD and do it now.

Church Folks Christians
Which One Are You or Both?

We are not in church for a competition; we are not on the Basketball Court or on a Football Field, a Golf Course or Tennis Court. Some of you are more serious, Church folks and Christians with the sports attire than paying your tithes in the church. Something is wrong with this picture! Can you tell me what it is? GOD is not through with any of us yet. Church is not a business. Church should be a place of worshipand peace. There is a saying that says that you can be in the Church and still not be there. Church folks/Christians and Pastors and Preachers etc., you fall under this same category. Please don't take advantage, stop taking advantage of the young people that's just coming into the church and Christ. They don't fully understand, just a Babe in Christ. Those who are disrespecting whom GOD put in place, please think before you do anything stupid. Please LORD; help those who know better to do better.

There were times when the Church Folks/Christians would have meetings to get rid of the Pastor. I don't want any part of this. If you would ask them individually what has the Pas- tor done to you for you to want to get rid of him or her? The person would not be able to answer truthfully or look you in the face.

What's the matter with Jesus, he's alright! What's the mat- ter with the Church Folks and Christians? You got to kneel at the cross. All of us go through things in life. The reason we go through different trials and tests is to get us closer. We are not even close there yet. Church Folks/Christians trying to tell another how to live their life when yours is blemish with a lot of foolishness.

Church Folks Christians
Which One Are You or Both?

I've visited a few Churches and the question was asked "If the LORD would come to get you right now would you be ready" please stand. A lot of people stood up and I said y'all standing know good and well you're not ready. I was sitting down they look at me. Y'all know what I know you better take a seat. That is exactly why, some of you are still here because you still have a few things to get prepared for. Get your houses in order meaning your heart. I just watch that person ask you for $1.00 and you hesitated. Yes, I gave the person $5.00 what they did with it was none of my business. I was placed where I was for such a time as this.

If you don't feel right in giving, don't give. If you go before a just God and he ask you why you didn't do this orthat. Don't get confuse when he say "Sorry, you didn't make it in because of your shortcomings. I'm pretty sure someone gave you from time to time. Do you have amnesia? Church Folks/ Christians some of you may get an attitude but, it is alright with me. I am only writing the truth.

We may have a death in the community according to whom it is, Christians and Church Folks may go all out for the pillar in the community. Someone else may die and Christians or Church Folks may show out with less than what the other person received. But again, Church Folks/Christians will have to give account. No matter who you are, everyone should get the same treatment. No little you and big me or big you and little me. Some Pastor's in the community, some Christians/ Church Folks may go all out for this particular Pastor but another Pastor may come through and they won't do anything for. GOD is not pleased with any of this.

Some of you may doubt some of what is going on but it is so true. Why do some people feel they were called to preach and not pick peaches. Christians/Church Folks need to take a step back and ask themselves rather or not they were called. I am not writing this

Church Folks Christians
Which One Are You or Both?

book to put anyone down. You need, I need to take a full inventory of our well-being. Are we doing all that the LORD want us to do. Why do some Church Folks/Christians have children and out of all they have one child would be treated better than the others. We have to give account for what we do.

Church Folks Christians
Which One Are You or Both?

Don't be so quick to put judgement on someone other than yourself. What gives you the right to judge people for what they do. There is no one living on earth perfect. If you think that you're living a perfect life you are a liar and the truth can't find you. We have to watch what we do. They're people and children watching every step we make . Church Folks/ Christians if you go to church and someone is preaching you think can't preach in the future if you know ahead you would rather stay home.

No matter how many people like you that will not get you in the kingdom. Church Folks and Christians would rather support some and not others then call and tell a lie about why they can't come to support you. God knows all about it. There is no need to lie to me. I am so glad that I don't entertain clicks either you like me or you don't. I really don't care. I don't live for people. I have the gift of seeing people for who they are and I know when they are lying. Christians and Church Folks, you tell people that you are through with me but if something hap- pens to you, you call me to let me know. Again, I don't entertain foolishness. I shall keep you in prayer though because you are in denial.

Please remember that God knows all and he sees all so please go run and tell that in case your memory is fooling you. The Lord is talking to us loud and clear but we are not listening or paying attention. We are too busy minding other folks business. On the phone or Facebook chatting. Girl so and so daughter is pregnant she didn't talk that though. Girl, did you hear about the Church Folk and Christian is sleeping around with the Deacon.

That child really needs to get out the pulpit she is not fooling anyone but herself. Leave it alone, the Lord already knows about it. Church Folks and Christians these trash is none of your business. You know that garbage but can I ask you a question who are you sleeping with? I don't want to hear it. I am moving right along.

Church Folks Christians
Which One Are You or Both?

A comment was made "That is sad when your Pastor is disrespectful, so sad, it turns you away from religion, sad, and say it isn't so, very sad! Bad part is there are so manydisrespectful men/women of the cloth these days it makes you wonder what GOD are they serving? A lot of these Pastors think they will make it to Heaven.

They are some people that attend church either they come in early or late or by the end of church they're gone once the church doors is open. Leaving before they can talk to anyone. This is not a Christian way to act. This is not friendly and please don't say I don't want to interact with the Church Folks. I just hope that you get it right. To be a "Christian" you must be nicer than you are.

You can be in the grocery store or clothing store or anywhere and see someone that you normally socialize with, but at this particular time you feel like you don't want to be bothered.Not even someone I go to church with, am I a Church Folk or a Christian? Answer Church Folk because, after you saw the person you could've said Hello and then keep it moving. No one should have to tell you whether you are a Church folk or a Christian. If you are true to yourself, you know that you can also be so phony and in that case you need to have a talk with Jesus. You know exactly what you are doing. You are not a person with Alzheimer's.

Some Church Folks/Christians are members of a church and they're not the Pastor. If God called you, he will give you an assignment to do . God will not tell you to disrespect the Pastor, leader of the Church. If things don't go your way, it is okay. How some Church Folks/Christians can see some people flaws but can't see their own. Some of the young kids go to church today because their mom and dad tell them to go. A lot of kids are disrespectful to their elders but it is not their fault, this is how they were raised. Don't let anyone talk to you in this or that kind of way or anyway. And you are not to disrespect someone older than you.

Church Folks Christians
Which One Are You or Both?

This is not a sweep around your own front door before you sweep around mines epic. This is a lesson in truth it hurts if you have a heart it will probably roll off your back like water (sweat).

Religion is not a Have and Have Not situation. We pray for all and then all of us have. How about that? The word for today is "To Share!

GOD is Love!

Do you know what LOVE is? I hear the words, What's Love Got to do With This? Well, love is what brought you into the world. Nowadays, it is called Lust.

Church Folks/Christians stop judging the young generation. Remember when you were their age. Everyone have a past that they want to leave in the past. I spoke to two (2) young men today at work and it almost brought me to tears. One young man said that when his father died, the preacher of the church he was attending wanted him to rent a limousine for him to ride in to the funeral and the gravesite. I have never heard anything like this in my life.

There was another time when he wasn't working and he caught odd jobs at the church. When he got a job, the Pastor told him that he had to pay all the months of tithes he owed when he wasn't really working. This guy did what he was told to do and then he decided to leave this church because of the Pastor's attitude towards him. He hasn't really gone to another church since because of the way the Pastor treated him. He feels scared. I am pretty sure I will talk to him about this again. I felt as though the Lord didn't want me to pressure this person at this time. This pastor really did a job on this young man. This young man does read though so he knows right and wrong.

Church Folks Christians
Which One Are You or Both?

Another man I spoke to I had him figured wrong, but I kept my opinions to myself. I told him that I am an author and I mentioned what my next book was about and I opened up some things because he just opened up to me just like that. He told me he had visited all types of Churches but he prefers the Pentecostal. I went to church where the people treat you like robots. They want to tell you who you can talk to and who you can't talk to and who you can't talk to. We have a family friend who is gay and he looked out for my daughter when she was away from home. He is like an adopted child; the church feels as though we should abandon him because he was gay. The guy told me before I remove this person from my life I would leave the church. God is love and I don't feel any love here at all.

Church folks/Christians where is the love in making someone feel bad for doing something good? Not everyone is for you Church folks/ Christian. We have to be very careful how we treat people when they come to our church to visit. We welcome them but, do we really mean it? If you have a particular seat in the church and you happen to come to church late, don't tell the person you need to move that is my seat. The only seat you should be worrying about should be a seat in the kingdom not in the pew.

Your pastor can't make a deal with you that you will be going to Heaven when he/she dies. Church folks/Christians don't know if they will get there. If you did someone wrong feel free to apologize it is okay to say that you are sorry. This works both ways.

Church folks versus Christians don't be deceived they are not the same. Church folks tear down other members and Christians build-up everyone they meet. Church folks act like they are happy for successes and Christians really are actually happy for you success. Church folks are extremely critical.

Church Folks Christians
Which One Are You or Both?

1 Peter 4:10-11. God has given each of us a gift from his great variety of spiritual gifts.

A true Christian has very long suffering and can deal with anything or anyone that comes their way. True Christians are kind and humble. Christians are not envy, jealous, prideful nor puffed up. Christians does not run from the truth or correction. Christians is very forbearing. Christians endure during hard trials. Christians put on clothes and you should put on Christ every day.

Church folks characteristics – examine us to be better in life. True influence behind the church folk's spirit.Ephesians 6:12 and 1 John4:11

Church folks: full of pride, strife and debate; strife – angry or bitter, disagreement, over fundamental issues andconflict. Bible version of strife- that terrible evil spirit that creates an atmosphere of anger that hangs just below the surface.Church folks: constantly murmur, very dogmatic, answer not good enough, subjective, cynical, conjectural and surmising, suppose that something is true without having evidence to confirm it, they need proof. A church folk always possesses a defined look and attitude. They are set in ways, are very harsh, stay separated from others because of different opinions, and are always in denial you can't tell them anything, they know everything.

Condemnation calls out faults never offer prayer and Convic- tion offers help and prayers. I've learned that on this earth no one is really a Christian, they all are Church folks.

Church folks have particular favors that they do for special people in the streets. I don't know of any Christians do you? I am who I am. God made me and he knows all about me. I don't have to lie nor procrastinate. If telling the truth is a gift Thank You Lord for the gift. I will continue to magnify his name and I am a church folk but so are you. When you findout who you are and where you are going, please let me know. No, let yourself know.

Church Folks Christians
Which One Are You or Both?

Church folks, you can go to church 7 days a week, 24 hours a day. Are you going because the church door is open or because it is just fashionable? GOD knows your reason. When you have your talk with Jesus you can't lie to him because, he knows it all so don't try pulling the wool over his eyes. The joke is really on you with the lies and backstabbing.

Church folks worrying about people in other states when they're not worried about their neighbors at home. I am not saying that you should not help because when we were in that predicament, we got help from everywhere and I would help also. Home is my first priority. You have some church folks that won't help with anything or help anyone. I find this to be very selfish. The saying that says what goes around comes back around. We need to show love better than we do. I just pray that we would be a better group of church folks that we can be. When we get together, Oh what a time we are going to have in the mighty name of Jesus!

Church folks/Christians there is a God that knows it all. There is nothing fabricated, false, or unreal. The Lord does not and will not make any mistakes. Yes, Jesus loves me he is all about love. He gave his only begotten son. People are truly something peculiar not to mention those that call themselves Christians.

A lot of people are sensitive in the church where they get offended when someone talks about their Pastor. Well, it is better you don't get tied up in the lives of these Pastors/Man of the cloth. The only person that you need to connect yourself to is the Holy Spirit that comes directly with Lord in mind.

Church Folks Christians
Which One Are You or Both?

Church folks/Christians will let you down some of them, so keep your guard up at all times so that you don't get hurt. They will promise you something and turn it around for their good which is sometimes bad. Church folks/Christians we are supposed to support each other. This is what the Lord would love for us to do. We have Church folks/Christians telling us who we can support and who we can't. The Lord don't invest in cults and people controlling people in such a manner. We as Church folks/Christians we have a mind of our own.Let's use it wisely. They're people out there with Alzheimer's/ Dementia one in the same that has a mind but lack stability of how to use it. This is not you. In this predicament we go from adult to child stages all over again. We are losing control day in and day out.

Love the Lord with all your heart. You know right from wrong. Being in the pulpit don't always make right. We still have crosses to bear. We still have to consult the Lord in our decisions. Some of us think, this is the mentality we should have, you better pray about it because that's not true in anyway. Get your own house in order before you preach on someone who told you something in confidence. You thought it was a perfect fit for your next sermon. Some of you saying if my Pastor leave the church we're out then will follow him or her. You better mind who you follow. Talk to the Lord in making these strong decisions.

We are not put on this earth to judge people. Sweep around your own front door. In other words travel with a mirror inyour pocket or purse at all times, why to examine yourself. They're people Church folks/Christians in the church not speaking to the other person for one reason or another. There is a reason and the door swings both in and out so it's not the person's problem/fault. Pastor's not talking to each other one reason or another. None of this should be happening not in the house of God. Preachers all I can say is Preach the word and have a seat unless the Holy Spirit directs your steps.

Church Folks Christians
Which One Are You or Both?

Church folks/ Christians don't think that the Lord is only directing your Pastor. Each of us has flaws. If you need to ask someone's forgiveness please do this vice/versa you can't make it in with malice in your heart. If you want to make it in I advise you to get it right. All of us need to get right with God. Some church folks are sweet and very caring, some are mean and spiteful.

Neither a tear drop nor a sigh. I am speechless yet I am still confused at how things occur and we still let go like nothing has happened at all. I tend to wonder sometimes if we live in a world all by ourselves.

What is gold-digger whereas you talk about a person like all they want from a person is what they can get from them and nothing more such as money or materialistic things.

Some of us are so darn selfish we think the sun come up when we rise or the moon goes in when we have completed our day. To hell with everyone else. With that mentality of foolishness said to turn false conceptions only thought by you. Your thinking is so small but your thoughts should be larger.

In life you think you are smarter than a teenager but our think- ing is totally different. We were born in different eras and things have definitely changed. Some people go to sleep and they're sleeping but testing your thought-process. They're not dead but yet, they have no feelings for no one but themselves. These are selfish human beings and they don't give a darn about no one else.

    I didn't come here by myself the Lord brought me here. The Lord knows and he see everything. There is nowhere that we can hide from the Master.

Church Folks Christians
Which One Are You or Both?

When someone in the street comes to you and asks for change or something to eat, you either turn your head or turn the other way and walk away. That was a test sent your way and you failed. Sometimes we eat, why can't I get a blessing, you just gave it away. It is not about us. The Church folk orthe so called Christians neither one of them can get you into the kingdom. Some of us are so selfish. We are jealous and why? The same God that bless some will bless others when it's their turn. Be grateful and thankful for the next person and watch God move.

Church folks/ so called Christians all of us need to get it together. We pray, we do a lot of things that we shouldn't do. Praise God from whom all blessings flow so blessings will flow all over the world. Why are we selfish? We don't know, we only think we suppose to help our own and no one else. As the Lord bless us, we are supposed to help others.

Christian (so called) and Church Folks before we share our food with others, we would rather give it to the dogs. Instead of us pass the clothes down to another child from you and your children, you would rather sell it to get money.

I am in a group that feeds the homeless. A friend of mine called and asked me if I would like to help and I said sure. The Lord has called her on home to be with him but, we are still doing it in her loving name and in her Honor. When you ask people to help, they have so much negative stuff to say. We leave them alone. We pray in our girls honor before we feed the meal. The people that we served they're so appreciative. Some of them have not always had it hard but because of the economy and hardship, they're here. We praise the Lord for being able to help. People will make excuses about them not helping. Thanks for the excuse but we say Thanks anyway. You go out to these expensive restaurants, order these lavish meals but yet, you can't contribute to a homeless person's meal.

Church Folks Christians
Which One Are You or Both?

Yes, we know that it is your money that you worked for but who helped you to make that money. I am not here to argue with you about your money. As the Lord bless us we should bless others. That is all, I have to say about that. I praise God for you.

When the Church folks or Christians(so called) looks at you like something is wrong with you, don't worry about it. The Lord has you in his plans and he knows exactly what his plans are for you. The Church folks are supposed to be there for us at all times. You say but, they're not, it's okay. The LORD is there for you all the time. He has an open ear, he listens when you talk to him and when you are silent, he still hears your cries, and he see your tears.

Why would a person of the cloth tell a person to bring their Pastor out to an open shame. Spread rumors about the Pastor and call the Superintendent on the Pastor. I am so embarrass to even be associated with such an angry and mean people.

How can you live with yourself getting a thrill hurting the person and you don't believe that you are doing anything wrong. How can you think, that you are going to enter the gate hurting someone and bragging about it. How can you be allowed to have kids in your home?

God is no way please with this foolishness. The Lord is so tired with all of us with all of these churches and all of these different denominations. He wants all of us to come together in love. He does not dwell in this foolishness.

Church Folks Christians
Which One Are You or Both?

He sends storms to get us straight. Most of us fails because we try to fix things instead of letting him handle them. Now, we have a much bigger issue. People are dying from this thing called Coronavirus. People like myself that has conditions such as Asthma, Diabetes and Heart Problems need to stay covered under the Blood. This thing is real. Please let's not take it lightly. People stay safe and encouraged. I see on Facebook pages, people shouting and putting on a show for when this pandemic is over how they're going to enter in church.

First of all Church is your heart. We all gather in a building and all of our hearts are not together where the Lord wants us to be. I don't care for selfish prayers because it means that we are selfish. Some of you don't understand that we don't need an audience to "Praise the Lord"!

This pandemic is a wake-up call. All of us need to wake the hell up. Everyone/Everybody wants to be a Preacher and you are not even a good Preacher. Your life is in disarray and your attitude stinks even though you put your good on the outside, trying to fake the crap. Have you fed the hungry?

Do you love yourself? Do you love people in general? Have you visited the sick and shut-in? How are your members doing if you are a Pastor of a Church?

Going back into the Church house are you going to find time to feed the homeless, are you going to find time to go and visit the sick and shut-in whether it be at their residence, the hospital or nursing home. You are always busy doing God's work.

We are going to have a service where you come as you are without the pretense. You can leave your heels at home or bring along some flats. We are going to learn how to really use our heart for the good and not the bad.

www.ingramcontent.com/pod-product-compliance
Lightning Source LLC
LaVergne TN
LVHW092008090526
838202LV00001B/48